MW01241296

TH

DRAGON MANUAL

The Best and Complete Pet owner's Manual on how to keep, train and raise a healthy Bearded Dragon

ELENA CRUZ

Table of Contents

CHAPTER ONE

INTRODUCTION

The Bearded dragon (Pogona vitticeps) may be a terrestrial, omnivorous, diurnal lizard native to Australia. Bearded dragons, additionally referred to as beardies, ar one among the foremost common lizards to stay as pets. Adults usually average lengths of 46-56 cm and weigh 300-500 grams.

A variety of color variations, or "morphs," are out there .

Bearded dragons could perform "head bobbing" and "arm-waving" behaviors. These displays will mean various things betting on the social scenario.

A beardie's beard will amendment color betting on his/her mood. Aggressive or agitated bearded dragons cantypically show a black beard.

With correct care, a bearded dragon will simply experience ten years.

CHAPTER TWO

BEARDED DRAGON HABITAT

A juvenile bearded dragon ought to be housed in a very ten gallon glass storage tank tank. The tank size can ought to increase because the beardie grows. Adults need a 20-50 gallon long glass storage tank tank. as a result of beardies like to climb, offer vertical area with va rious branches.

BEARDED DRAGON SUBSTRATE

The safest and best substrates to use ar paper, newspaper, towel, or slate. If you favor a a lot of representational look, associate with slate. "Reptile Carpet" will be used, however should be modifi ed and washed (preferably in a very washer with detergent) a minimum of weekly. Alfalfa-based rabbit pellets also can be used; they're safe if accidentally eaten, and facilitate absorb odor. However, the pellets disintegrate and mildew if they get wet, therefore you cannot have a water dish within the enclosure if you're victimisation pellets. Instead, you'dought to soak your bearded dragon double weekly to confirm that he/she is obtaining adequate water.

Aquarium gravel, walnut shells, metallic element sand, and natural sand don't seem to be suggested, thanks to the chance of internal organ impactions if enclosed.

CHAPTER THREE

HEAT REQUIREMENT IN BEARDED DRAGONS

It is important to produce a gradient for your bearded dragon to permit him/her to control its own blood heat. the nice and cozy finish of the enclosure ought to be maintained at 80-90°F, with the other aspect of the cage from 75-80° F. A basking spot of 100-115°F ought to even be provided by transcription a ascent branch or rock 8-12"beneath the warmth supply.

There ar many other ways to produce correct heat. we have a tendency to suggest employing a mercury vapor bulb to produce each full spectrum ultraviolet {light warmth to your bearded dragon. this could be left on a minimum of twelve hours per day. At night, we have a tendency to suggest employing a 60-100 watt Ceramic Heat electrode bulb, which is able to provide off heat while not lightweight, to take care of acceptable enclosure temperatures.

Depending on your house temperature, you'll additionally w ant some under-tank heating. many sorts of heating pads/heat tape ar out there at pet stores and on-line. If AN under-tank heater is employed, it's important to buy a top quality thermostat to assist management the warmth output and maintain safe and acceptable temperatures.

Do not use heat rocks! These usually can overheat, inflicti ng burns to reptiles and making a fireplace hazard.

The enclosure temperature ought to be monitored closely with AN correct measuring instrument to
create positivethat it's staying with in the "optimum temperature zone" for you r pet. we have a tendency to suggest victimization temperature guns or probe thermometers in order that the particular temperature of the cage floor or basking spotwill be accurately measured. Dial or

tape thermometers placed on the wall of the enclosure don't accurately mirrort the temperatures your pet is experiencing.

CHAPTER FOUR
PROVIDING LIGHT FOR YOUR BEARDED DRAGONS

UV lightweight exposure is crucial for maintaining a healthy bearded dragon. Adequate exposure to full spectrum Ultraviolet light is important for generation of victuals

D3, that is successively important to the flexibility of the beardie to soak up metallic element. Direct natural daylight ought to be supplemented whenever doable. bear in mind that windows filter ultraviolet |ultraviolet illuminationUV actinic radiation light, therefore obtaining daylight through a window isn't adequate.

Bearded dragons ought to receive twelve hours of ultraviolet light lighting daily. If it's a sunny, warm day, we have a tendency to suggest taking your bearded dragon outside for natural daylight exposure. There are some nice sunning cages out there, otherwise you will build an easy cage with window screens. make certain that a number of shade is often out there, and maximize the air flow.

If you're unable to produce natural daylight, you may got to offer the UVB through artificial lighting. Mercury vapor bulbs ar presently the simplest supply for artificial ultraviolet light ultra violet |actinic radiation actinic ray} light on the market, and are our high recommendation for bearded dragons. instead, a 10.0 fluorescent bulb will be used.

It is vital to notice that fluorescent ultraviolet light lights can stop manufacturing ultraviolet light spectrum lighting long before they stop manufacturing actinic ray. As a result, we have a tendency to suggest substitution the bulbs each 4-6 months.

CHAPTER FIVE
BEARDED DRAGONS DIET

Bearded dragons are omnivorous within the wild. Therefore, they must be offered vegetables, fruits, and insects in their diet. Fruits ought to be unbroken to a minimum, focusing totally on vegetables and insects.

Juveniles: supply insects within the evening and a cut tossed salad within the morning. Purchased hatchlings ought to be pronto intake salad/vegetabl es, however if insects ar gift, the lizards typically won't bit their vegetables. As salad/vegetables can conjure the bulk of the adult bearded dragon diet, it's important to start out exposing the babies at a young age to the present food. it's additionally sugg ested to stay moistened bearded dragon pelleted diet out there the least bit times.

Adults: Adult bearded dragons ought to receive

a cut tossed salad once daily, and insects 3 times weekly. A bearded dragon pelleted diet will be offered the least bit times.

More info on diet components:

Chopped inexperienced salad: sup ply a
combination of contemporary inex perienced vegetables and greens daily.
This may embrace kale, kale, parsley, leafy
vegetable, blowball greens,
plantain, cruciferous vegetable, escarole, and chicory. The bulk of your

greens combine ought to be composed of the higher than ingredients, however additionally add a number of the following: carrots (carrot peelings work great), yellow summer squash, butternut squash,inexperienced beans, dandelion, red clover, squash, hibiscus, and nasturtium blossoms.

Be sure to scrub any purchased greens, and make certain that you simply don't seem to be accidentally exposing your bearded dragon to chemicals or pesticides

if you're aggregation any of

those materials yourself. The mix will be cut in a very kitchen appliance or hand cut and keep within the white goods for up to per week.the combo may be frozen in little batches and thawed before feeding. Some beardies that ar at home with contemporary greens might not pronto eat pre-frozen food. Occasional fruit items, like orange, mango, banana, or apple, is also offered no over once weekly. Insects: we have a tendency to suggest feeding mealworms and cockroaches because the insect portion of the diet, mixed with different insects to produce selection (butterworms, hornworms, superworms, waxworms, phoenix worms, and crickets). Feed as several insects because the beardie can consume among a sitting. make certain that the insect prey is fitly sized for your beardie. The insects shouldn't be larger than the dimension of the bearded dragon's head. These insects ought to be "gutloaded", or fed a whole, correct diet for a minimum of 24-48 hours before feeding them to your bearded dragon. a decent basic diet for gut loading insects is layer chicken pellets supplemented with contemporary fruits and vegetables. mixture softened pellets with greens is usually recommended.

It is vital to notice that bearded dragon pellets don't seem to be a whole diet. each insects and vegetables should even be fed to stay your beardie healthy!

CHAPTER SIX
BEARDED DRAGONS DIET
SUPPLEMENTATION

Lack of acceptable supplementation will result in serious health issues in bearded dragons, as well as skeletal deformities and organ failure.

Both the insects and therefore the salad/vegetables ought

to be dirted with metallic element dust 4-5 days/week. The metallic element dirt ought to contain no chemical element or further vitamins.

Twice a month, a vertebrate multi-vitamin ought
to be accustomed dirt the
food things instead. don't supplem
ent with vitamins a lot of typically,
as fat soluble vitamins like fat-soluble vitamin and vitamin D will
be harmful if overdosed.

WATER REQUIREMENT IN BEARDED DRAGONS

Bearded dragons receive most of their necessary water from food (provided
that they're intake greens regularly). A water bowl should be given
 contemporary, clean water (unless you're victimisation pellet substrate). However, some beardies won't faithfully drink
from a water bowl. you'll facilitate make
certain your beardie stayshydrous by misting water onto his/her head or soaking the animal in lukewarm water double weekly.

HANDLING YOUR BEARDED DRAGONS

Every day, fastidiously develop your beardie and let it sit on your hand within the cage. permit it to go away your hand whenever it desires. this can permit your beardie get accustomed being command and discharged. mild daily handling can facilitate your bearded dragon become tame.

CHAPTER SEVEN
VETERINARY CARE IN BEARDED DRAGONS

I suggest acting annual to
bi-annual exams bearded dragons
as a preventative health live. an
intensive
communication permits our

veterinarians to catch health issues early, before they become a lot of serious. we have a tendency
to suggest acting regular dirty exams to visualize for parasites, and occasional bloodwork to assess general health.

COMMON HEALTH ISSUES IN BEARDED DRAGONS

*Nutritional secondary glandular disorder (metabolic bone disease) – caused by inappropriate dietary supplementation of metallic element

*Parasites – quite common in
bearded dragons

Atadenovirus –

 AN infectious infective
agent unwellness that affects the
central system, system,
and alimentary canal of affected
bearded dragons. several bearded
dragons ar carriers of this
virus. sadly, the infection will be
deadly, and there's presently no
cure.

*Obesity – usually happens in
bearded dragons
that ar intake inappropriate,
excessive diets and not receiving

adequate   exercise.

*Dysecdysis –
 issues with traditional shedding, t
ypically caused   by
inappropriate humidness

*Trauma – from deterioration of
cage furnishings, being born, or
being   attacked   by different pets
Impactions – typically caused by a
mix of   poor agriculture and
inappropriate substrate selections.

CHAPTER EIGHT

HOW TO GO ABOUT WITH YOUR BEARDED DRAGONS HOME

Once your pet is big, you'll desire a glass vivarium of a   minimum of forty gallons   in   volume (that's thirty   two to thirty sixinches long) with a screened lid for him to measure in. Your bearded dragon is from a heat, dry surroundings thusyou'll additionally want a heating supply for his home. Your dragon prefers the solitary life.

What am i able to place in my bearded dragon's terrarium? To inform him of the desert of his ancestors, line the lowest of your bearded

dragon's vivarium with 2 to a few inches of atomic number 20 sand, or invest in reptilian carpet. Carpet could be a better option for younger bearded dragons. take

away waste a   minimum
of once per week, and treat him
to contemporary bedding once a
month.

Reptiles may
be fastidious concerning comfy te
mperature. make   sure to
offer your   bearded   dragon a
bit of woodor   rock,   to   climb a
bit nearer to his heat supply, or to
cover behind.   Add a   number
of branches
for concealmentand ascent.

HEATING & LIGHTING
ESSENTIAL TIPS

Bearded dragons square measure ectotherms. which means they'll want each a reliable supply of warmth and a cooler space to remain comfortable. Here square measure some a lot of tips about heating and lighting to stay in mind:

• Your dragon's home ground ought to have a measuring

instrument at every finish, further as a hygrometer—a device that measures wetness. Your bearded dragon thrives once wetness is between two hundredth and half-hour.

• If wetness is a smaller amount than two hundredth, a lightweight misting once day is spare.

• Place your heat light-weight over the basking spot, that ought to be the warmest space within the home groundthroughout the day: a hundred to one hundred ten degrees Gabriel Daniel Fahrenheit (38 to forty nine Centigrade). The

cool finish ought
to be concerning seventy
five to eighty five F (24 to twenty
nine C).

• Turn the basking light-weight off at nighttime. Use a ceramic heat electrode or night electric heater to stay the temperature between sixty six and seventy five degrees F (18 to twenty four C).

• Bearded dragons square measure active throughout day
and sleep at nighttime — similar to you. Unlike you, they like basking underneath a UVA/UVB

bulb

for concerning twelve hours every day.

• For night viewing, switch to a night-specific   bulb to stay from worrisome your bearded dragon

BEARDED   DRAGONS FEEDING   TIPS

Bearded   dragons eat each plants and   meat. Feed your bearded dragon 2 to a few times each day. A

young offspring can largely eat tin y insects. However once   your bearded dragon could be a bit a lot of mature, he'll get pleasure from vegetables, too. certify to scrub his water and food bowl often.

• Insects: crickets, mealworms and wax worms, dirt with atomic number

20 supplement doubly weekly

•

Vegetables: shredded dark foliose greens or carrots fed each different

BEARDED DRAGONS HEALTH CARE TIPS

Try to not handle your new reptilian for 3 or four days — they have an opportunity to urge accustomed their new home. Even a settled-in lizard will feel sick — if you notice any of those symptoms, it would be an honest time to go to the vet:

• More concealment time than usual

• Less intake and drinking, perhaps even weight loss

• Swollen joints

• Skin is stained and shedding

• Discharge from the eyes, nose or mouth

• Droppings that look liquid for over 2 days

PET SAFETY TIPS

• All pets

will doubtless carry infective agent, bacterial, fungal, and parasitic diseases contagious to humans.

• Thoroughly wash your hands with heat, cleaner water before and once contact with any pet or its home ground.

• Adults ought to assist youngsters with hand laundry once contact with a pet, its home ground or storage tank water.

To start your relationship along with your dragon, you wish to possess associate degree ample enclosure with a spread of rocks and wood to explore. As well, you wish to possess a spread of meats, veggies, greens and fruit to stay them happy. Any pet can trust and "play" with you once they understand you're providing what they have.

Because they're therefore docile, beardies can permit you to handle them, however like several pet, some don'tsort of a ton of touching. The a lot of you're employed with them, the a lot of they'll trust you. after you handle them, they like peaceful

surroundings, therefore certify there's not plenty of activity with alternative pets or individuals around your dragon.

Unlike alternative lizards, bearded dragons cannot regenerate lost tails or limbs, therefore be containerful and decide them up by their tails. Be mild with them so they are doing not become frightened and take a look at to leap away and escape.

Do not show concern or hesitation; with confidence scoop them up in your hand so you're supporting their entire body, together with the legs and tail. they are doing not like being picked up from the highest, therefore decide them up from the aspect or beneath.

The younger your beardie is, the a lot of careful you've got to be, as young ones frighten a lot of simply and should hiss at you. Again, don't show concern, be assured and be safe. whether or not your dragon is younger or older, don't handle them for long periods of your time as this will produce stress. Handle them a lot of oft for shorter periods of your time and that they can become a lot of acceptive of you.

You want to start obtaining your beardie accustomed you by taming them right away. don't wait or hesitate. If they show signs of aggression, hold them firmly with each hands and pet them oft. If they're overtly aggressive,allow them to select a brief whereas and handle them a lot of oft till they cool down. If they're terribly aggressive, the taming method could take many w eeks, however keep at it and you may have a rewardful pet dragon.

As you handle your beardie, you wish to apply correct hygiene and wash your hands when handling. this can be very

true with youngsters. ne'er bit you r face or food till you've got washed your hands as Bearded Dragons, like all lizards, will carry micro organism|enterobacteria|enterics} bacteria on their skin. this will offer you a nastymalady, therefore certify you wash your hands.

Salmonella bacterium will cause severe stomachaches with plenty of cramping, diarrhea, ejection and high temperatures. It will last for over per week if you don't see your doctor, then it'll still take it slow to recover. So again, the easy hindrance is to clean your hands.

If there square measure youngsters around, certif

y your beardies enclosure is secured properly so there's adultsupervising the least bit times. As well, place away all provides and food things to decrease the prospect of a toddler obtaining sick or your beardie being injured.

Giving your dragon a bit freedom is nice, however certify it's restricted and supervised. ne'er allow them to in yourroom or anyplace that you simply serve food or eat – assume the TV and games space here.

Your Bearded Dragons care may appear overwhelming initially, ho wever it's constant with several ne w pets. These dragons square measure fun to

possess, fascinating to look at, and with correct care and handling, will offer you and your family a few years of enjoyment

CHAPTER NINE

YOU NEED A HEALTHY BEARDED DRAGON

Choosing a healthy, well started animal to start with is probably the only nonetheless most significant facet ofthriving bearded dragon rearing. whereas it's unlikely that any dealer would deliberately supply unsuita ble .babies purchasable, it's still an honest plan to understand the way to spot a healthy specimen.

The animal ought to be alert and alert to physical stimuli. Most baby bearded dragons can sit placidly within the palm of ones hand, and this is often fine. However, you must be ready to notice a particular quantity of resistance and tone within the lizard as you decide it up.

The eyes ought to be wide open, of equal size, and show no signs of infection (mucous, crusts, etc.). The mouth and nares ought to be equally examined. Well fed bearded dragons ought to have a rounded out look. they must be plump with no visible hip or back bones.

Finally,   if choosing from an outsized cluster of   animals, look 1st at people   who are the most important and most active. These are generally the   "alpha" animals,   and are an excellent alternative. Once these animals are culled   from   the cluster, the smaller, less assertive ones can quickly placed   on size and   catch   up   with their additional dominant counterparts.

FEEDING   TIPS

Bearded dragons are quick
growing creatures with equally
speedy   metabolisms. to
confirm correct growth,   and to
scale back the danger of digit and
tail nipping among cage mates,
baby bearded dragons ought to be
fed always.

Appetites can vary from specimen

to specimen, however the common growing bearded dragon can thirstily eatthree times daily, with every feeding consisting of but several crickets the animal consumes in a very fifteen minute amount. this is often AN optimum feeding regime , one usually utilized by breeders and advanced hobbyists to induce their animals up to size as quickly as attainable.

In some cases, providing crickets three tim es daily isn't sensible for the keeper. luckily, animals can still thrive on a less intensive feeding schedule, the sole side-effect being a

rather slower rate. additional usually than not, baby bearded dragons will be offered live prey once or double daily (along with recent greens) with no issues.

Food things ought to be now not than the gap between the lizards eyes. Feeding large of prey could be a frequent side effect, and may result in serious health issues. once unsure, perpetually supply a

bigger amount of little prey

things rather than a little range of larger ones. moreover, don't feed mealworms to bearded dragons but four months more matured. Smaller animals typically, although not perpetually, have hassle digesting the robust,polysaccharide shell of the worms.

All foods, each live and otherwise, ought to be gently dusted with a prime quality Ca and nutriment supplement. The Ca supplement chosen ought to be one complete with nutriment D3.
This nutriment, in conjunction with correct heat and light-weight, can aid greatly is

preventing metabolic disorders. This calcium/D3 supplement ought to be used at each feeding till the animal has reached maturity, at which era it's use could also be safely reduced.

A vertebrate vitamin pill ought to be used furthermore, though is merely necessary once or double per week. Thelarge choice of vitamins and minerals found within the recent vegetables being eaten can give for abundant of the animals wants. the utilization of an

extra supplement is just a fail safe, ought to the choice of turn out be deficient in one or additional essential nutrients.

HANDLING TIPS IN BEARDED DRAGONS

One final pitfall that a lot of 1st time vertebrate keepers encounter is stressed animals as a results of over handling. like any vertebrate, ever y individual can have variable tole rances for human contact.

Fortunately bearded dragons as a full ar rather content to be picked up and interacted with on a daily basis. still, one ought to begin slowly, permitting a brand new baby bearded ample time to adjust each to its new surroundings and to human contact.

Keep in mind that baby bearded dragons ar simply that,
babies. they're experiencing several things for the primarytime and may simply become flooded or frightened. it's for these reasons that handling ought to be unbroken to a minimum till the animal has had ample time to settle in.

Once the lizard has begun

feeding often and seems to be exhibiting traditional behavioural patterns, regular handling could start. it's best to begin slowly, gently lifting the animal into the palm and permitting it to take a seat, unrestrained, for a couple of moments. Over time young beardeds can begin to grasp that humans mean them no hurt, and most can, by one year more matured, be fully comfy sitting on ones shoulder or being hand fed.

THE END

Made in the USA
Middletown, DE
27 October 2021

51121595R00038